CORE LIBRARY OF US STATES

New Hampshire

abdobooks.com

Published by Abdo Publishing, a division of ABDO, PO Box 398166, Minneapolis, Minnesota 55439.
Copyright © 2023 by Abdo Consulting Group, Inc. International copyrights reserved in all countries.
No part of this book may be reproduced in any form without written permission from the publisher.
Core Library™ is a trademark and logo of Abdo Publishing.

Printed in the United States of America, North Mankato, Minnesota.
052022
092022

Cover Photo: Shutterstock Images
Interior Photos: Paul Tessier/Shutterstock Images, 4–5; Red Line Editorial, 7 (New Hampshire),
7 (USA); Rich Beauchesne/Portsmouth Herald/AP Images, 10–11, 43; Sean Pavone/Shutterstock
Images, 13, 26–27, 34–35, 45; iStockphoto, 15; Lukasz Stefanski/Shutterstock Images, 18 (flag); Tom
Reichner/Shutterstock Images, 18 (deer); Steve Byland/Shutterstock Images, 18 (bird); Kathleen
Riley/iStockphoto, 18 (dog); Shutterstock Images, 18 (flower), 29; James Kirkikis/Shutterstock
Images, 20–21; Lewis Wickes Hine/Library of Congress/Corbis Historical/VCG/Getty Images, 31;
C. O. Leong/Shutterstock Images, 32; Randy Duchaine/Alamy, 37; Pernelle Voyage/Shutterstock
Images, 39

Editor: Marie Pearson
Series Designer: Joshua Olson

Library of Congress Control Number: 2021951417

Publisher's Cataloging-in-Publication Data

Names: Conley, Kate, author.
Title: New Hampshire / by Kate Conley
Description: Minneapolis, Minnesota : Abdo Publishing, 2023 | Series: Core library of US states |
    Includes online resources and index.
Identifiers: ISBN 9781532197703 (lib. bdg.) | ISBN 9781098270469 (ebook)
Subjects: LCSH: U.S. states--Juvenile literature. | Northeastern States--Juvenile literature. | New
    Hampshire--History--Juvenile literature. | Physical geography--United States--Juvenile
    literature.
Classification: DDC 974.2--dc23

Population demographics broken down by race and ethnicity come from the 2019 census estimate.
Population totals come from the 2020 census.

CONTENTS

THE GRANITE
STATE

At dusk a group of people board a bus in Gorham, New Hampshire. As the sun sinks lower, they grow excited. The bus drives along the Androscoggin River. The passengers peer out the windows. A tour guide shines a spotlight out of the bus to see better. At last the guide sees what they have all been waiting for. A moose slowly walks out of the river. The people in the bus are in awe of its size and beauty.

Moose live throughout the state of New Hampshire.

And then, just as quickly as it appeared, the moose disappears into the dense forest.

Moose watching is just one of New Hampshire's many adventures. The state is known for its White Mountains. People go there to hike, canoe, and admire fall leaves. The state also has many lakes and rivers, as well as a shoreline along the coast.

PERSPECTIVES

YANKEES

People from New Hampshire and other parts of New England are often called Yankees. At first it was used in a negative way. In the 1700s British soldiers called colonists who rebelled "Yankees." But over time the meaning changed. It now represents the independent spirit of the people from the area. This also includes the values of being thrifty and shrewd. Today many New Englanders embrace the term.

ABOUT NEW HAMPSHIRE

New Hampshire is part of New England. This region is in the northeastern United States. Quebec, Canada, forms the state's

MAP OF
NEW HAMPSHIRE

Examine this map of New Hampshire. How do the locations on this map help you better understand Chapter One?

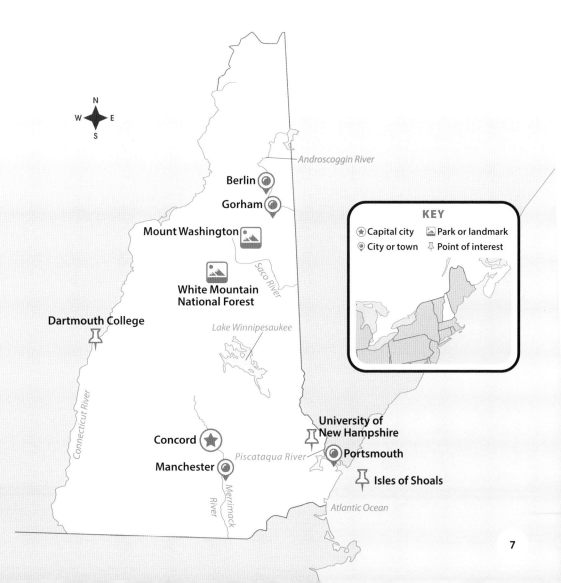

THE ABENAKI

Today fewer than 1,000 Abenaki still live in New Hampshire. But their presence in the state is represented in part by many place names. One example is the state's largest lake, known as Lake Winnipesaukee. In the Abenaki language, this name means "the lake between or around land or islands." The early Abenaki people in New Hampshire are also honored at the Strawbery Banke Museum. It has an exhibit called People of the Dawnland dedicated to the Abenaki. In 2021 museum staff joined with the Cowasuck Band of the Pennacook-Abenaki People to build a wigwam. It is a dome-shaped home historically used by the Abenaki.

northern border. To the east New Hampshire borders Maine and the Atlantic Ocean. It borders Vermont to the west. Massachusetts is to the south.

Concord is the capital of New Hampshire. It is a small, charming city on the Merrimack River. One of the goods it produces is granite. Granite is a rock common throughout New Hampshire. For that reason New Hampshire is known as the Granite State.

The Abenaki have lived in New Hampshire for thousands of years. Europeans first arrived in the early 1600s. They later established New Hampshire as an English colony. People of New Hampshire later joined together to fight for their independence from the British. Today New Hampshire remains an important part of the nation. It is a leader in business and manufacturing. Its rugged land is heavily forested and filled with wildlife. And its people have contributed to the nation in many ways, from visiting space to writing famous poems. All these factors make New Hampshire a place unlike any other.

EXPLORE ONLINE

Chapter One provides an overview of New Hampshire. The website below gives more information about the state. What new information does the article give?

NEW HAMPSHIRE

abdocorelibrary.com/new-hampshire

CHAPTER TWO

HISTORY OF NEW HAMPSHIRE

People have lived in New England for approximately 12,000 years. Eventually they formed several nations. The American Indian people of New Hampshire are the Abenaki. Their name means "People of the Dawnland." The Abenaki historically lived in villages along rivers and lakes. They hunted, farmed, and fished in the lands nearby. Abenaki people continue to live in the state.

In about 1507 an explorer named Sebastian Cabot sailed along the coast of

Some people keep alive the traditional Abenaki crafts, such as making birch-bark baskets.

New England. Although American Indian peoples already lived on this land, Cabot claimed it for the British. In 1603 Captain Martin Pring landed in present-day Portsmouth. Pring and his crew became the first Europeans known to set foot in New Hampshire.

After Pring's arrival more Europeans came to New Hampshire. In the early 1600s, Europeans exposed the Abenaki to diseases such as smallpox and measles. The Abenaki had no immunity to the diseases. Thousands died.

ESTABLISHING A COLONY

England's King James I wanted more people to settle in New England. He awarded land grants in the 1620s to form a British colony in the area. The settlers established small fishing villages. These included Strawbery Banke, which later became present-day Portsmouth.

In 1629 a large land grant went to a British colonel named John Mason. It covered the land between the Merrimack and Piscataqua Rivers. It ran from the coast

Water has played an important role in Portsmouth's economy since the city was founded.

to 60 miles (97 km) inland. Mason named the land New Hampshire after the area in England where he grew up. He brought a group of settlers there and started a fur trading business.

New Hampshire continued to grow in the 1700s. New cities were founded along the coast as trade grew. Farther inland, colonists cleared land for small farms. The need for new land caused fighting between the colonists and the Abenaki. By the 1740s colonists had pushed many of the remaining Abenaki out of

New Hampshire. Today there are a few tribes in the state, but none are federally recognized.

THE REVOLUTION

The colonists of New Hampshire believed strongly in local government. They valued independence. Beginning in the 1760s, this created a rising tension with the British. The British were in debt for wars they had been fighting. To pay off the debt, the British government began to charge the colonists high taxes. But the colonists had no one to represent their interests to the British government.

As tensions rose the British began to collect gunpowder and guns from British forts in the colonies. They did not want the colonists to have access to these items if a war began. In December 1774 Paul Revere rode from Boston to Portsmouth. He warned colonists that British forces planned to take the guns and gunpowder from the British fort William and Mary in New Castle. The next morning a group of New

Paul Revere lived from 1734 to 1818.

Hampshire colonists stormed the poorly guarded fort. They took 100 barrels of gunpowder.

These tensions led to the Revolutionary War (1775–1783). The war began in April 1775. New Hampshire was the only colony that did not have any battles on its soil. But it still played a large role in the revolution. It supplied many soldiers in the war effort. In January 1776 the people of New Hampshire adopted their own state constitution. It was the first of its kind in the nation.

The war ended in 1783, and the colonies gained their freedom. New Hampshire ratified the US Constitution on June 21, 1788. By doing so, enough states had approved the document to allow the Constitution to become the nation's official law. New Hampshire became the nation's ninth state.

STATEHOOD

In the early 1800s, the Industrial Age began in New Hampshire. People from the country began to move to the cities. There, newly created factories offered many jobs.

Later that century the United States entered the Civil War (1861–1865). Southern states fought to continue slavery. Northern states, called the Union, fought to keep the nation together and make slavery illegal. New Hampshire was part of the Union. About 35,000 soldiers from New Hampshire fought in the war. The state's factories produced shoes, uniforms, and guns for Union soldiers. Shipyards in Portsmouth made warships. The Union won the war in 1865.

In the following years, New Hampshire continued to develop. Immigrants from many parts of Europe arrived there to work in the factories. Cities grew larger. Farms became less common, and the state began to rely on tourism as an important part of its economy.

Today New Hampshire continues to thrive. It is run by three branches of government: legislative, executive, and judicial. The legislative branch makes the state's laws. It is known as the General Court of New Hampshire. The executive branch enacts the

NEW HAMPSHIRE
QUICK FACTS

Take a look at these facts and symbols of New Hampshire. How do you think each one is important to the state?

Abbreviation: NH
Nickname: The Granite State
Motto: Live free or die
Date of statehood: June 21, 1788
Capital: Concord
Population: 1,377,529
Area: 9,349 square miles (24,214 sq km)

STATE SYMBOLS

State animal
White-tailed deer

State dog
Chinook

State bird
Purple finch

State wildflower
Pink lady's-slipper

state's laws. The governor leads this branch. The judicial branch interprets the state's laws. This happens in the state's courts.

Residents stay true to the state's motto: Live Free or Die. For example, New Hampshire is one of the nation's few states that does not have an income tax or a sales tax. They are living free from paying those taxes. This draws businesses and residents alike to the state. New Hampshire continues to contribute much to the United States.

PRESIDENTIAL PRIMARY

Every four years the people of New Hampshire hold a presidential primary. A primary helps determine who will become the official candidates for US president. New Hampshire's primary receives lots of attention. That is because it is the first primary in the nation. Poor support in the primary can derail a candidate. Strong support can give momentum to the candidate. No president has won the election without coming in first or second in New Hampshire's primary.

GEOGRAPHY AND CLIMATE

Mountains cover the northern part of New Hampshire. Early colonists called them the White Mountains because of their snowy peaks. The White Mountains cover about one-third of New Hampshire. They contain the highest point in the state, Mount Washington. It rises 6,288 feet (1,917 m) above sea level.

South of the White Mountains, the state's land shifts to rolling hills. Scattered among the hills are the state's nearly 1,300 lakes

Some people enjoy ice fishing on Lake Winnipesaukee in the winter.

STATE EMBLEM

The Old Man of the Mountain was one of New Hampshire's most famous landmarks. This rock formation looked like the profile of a man. It became a symbol of the state. But the rock formation began to slowly erode. Scientists tried to keep it in place using iron rods and cables. But in May 2003, the rock formation crumbled, and the profile disappeared. Despite this, the Old Man of the Mountain remains New Hampshire's state emblem. It appears on license plates and road signs across the state.

and ponds. The largest is Lake Winnipesaukee. It has many bays and hundreds of islands. People visit resorts near the lake to swim, fish, and boat.

New Hampshire also has approximately 40 rivers. Sometimes New Hampshire is called the Mother of Rivers. That's because five of New England's major rivers start there. They are the Connecticut, the Piscataqua, the Androscoggin, the Merrimack, and the Saco Rivers.

In the southeast, New Hampshire has about 18 miles (29 km) of coastline along the Atlantic Ocean.

It is the shortest coastline of any state that borders an ocean. Six miles (9.7 km) off the coast is a group of nine rocky islands. They are called the Isles of Shoals. Four of the islands are part of New Hampshire. The remaining five belong to Maine.

CLIMATE

Like most of New England, New Hampshire has a temperate climate. Winters are cold and snowy. The state's mountains have the coolest temperatures, often dipping below 0 degrees Fahrenheit (−18°C). The mountains can receive up to 100 inches (250 cm)

PERSPECTIVES
SURVIVING WINTER

The snowy winters in New Hampshire's mountains can be harsh. When Tiffany Hale moved there from Michigan, she wasn't sure what to expect. But she was pleasantly surprised. "I was impressed with the way the community came together to help each other," said Hale in 2018. "On our local Facebook group I saw people offering each other rides to work, plowing driveways for the elderly free of charge."

of snow each year. The other parts of the state are a bit warmer. They receive much less snow.

Spring and summer bring warmer temperatures. In the mountains, the average temperature in July is between 75 and 80 degrees Fahrenheit (24° and 27°C). The rest of the state has an average temperature that is about 5 degrees Fahrenheit (2.8°C) warmer. Many tourists visit the state and explore its mountains and lakes during this time.

In the fall, temperatures begin to drop. Leaves on the trees begin to change colors. They turn shades of red, orange, and brown. Visitors flock to the state to see them.

PLANTS AND ANIMALS

New Hampshire is the second-most forested state behind Maine. Forests cover 81 percent of New Hampshire. Common trees include the red maple, the white pine, the hemlock, the balsam fir, and the sugar maple. The white birch is the state tree. It grows in all parts of the state. There are also shrubs such as blueberries, mountain laurels, and sumacs. Daisies, wild violets, and asters are common wildflowers. The state wildflower is the pink lady's-slipper. Its blossom is shaped much like a lady's slipper.

The state has a variety of animals. Forests are home to white-tailed deer, black bears, moose, and raccoons. The rivers and lakes have many kinds of fish, such as trout, bass, and perch. Birds include purple finches, owls, osprey, and turkeys. Shrimp, clams, and lobsters live in the coastal waters.

FURTHER EVIDENCE

Chapter Three discusses New Hampshire's geography. Identify one of the chapter's main points. Then visit the article at the website below. Does the information on the website support the main point of the chapter? Does it present new evidence?

NEW HAMPSHIRE GEOGRAPHY

abdocorelibrary.com/new-hampshire

CHAPTER
FOUR

RESOURCES AND ECONOMY

New Hampshire is full of natural resources. Fishing was an early part of the colony's economy. Its lakes and rivers teemed with salmon and shad. Waters off the coast had vast amounts of cod. The fish could be salted and dried to preserve them.

New Hampshire colonists also supplied the British with furs. The Abenaki knew where to hunt beavers. They provided the colonists with beaver pelts. In exchange

New Hampshire's waters continue to be a source of jobs as well as a place for recreation.

the colonists provided the Abenaki with goods such as guns, pots, and axes. Then the colonists sold the furs to the Europeans.

The forests were another important natural resource. Colonists cut down trees for lumber and sold it. The lumber was used to build homes, tools, ships, and more. The white pines of the forest could grow more than 150 feet (45 m) tall. This made them ideal for ship masts.

PERSPECTIVES

FARMS IN NEW HAMPSHIRE

Early settlers in New Hampshire often cleared land for small farms. To survive, colonists needed to grow their own food. Today farming makes up only a small part of the state's economy. Dairy products and plants grown in nurseries make up two-thirds of the state's farming output. Farmers also grow fruits and vegetables and raise livestock. In addition, some farmers tap maple trees to produce maple syrup.

THE INDUSTRIAL AGE

In the 1800s the economy in New Hampshire began to change. People began

New Hampshire's forests have made wood an important resource in the state.

building factories in the state. Factories were often built along rivers, which powered the factory machines. The machines allowed businesses to produce goods more quickly and cheaply than ever before. This era is known as the Industrial Age. New Hampshire was one of the nation's first states to have large-scale manufacturing. Many immigrants, including those from Russia, Italy, and Poland, also arrived during this time. They often took jobs in the factories.

GRANITE

New Hampshire has many granite formations and quarries. Granite is one of the state's natural resources. New Hampshire granite is exported throughout the world. Blocks of granite can be used to construct walls, bridges, buildings, and monuments. Crushed granite can be used to make driveways, paths, and roads.

Many of New Hampshire's early factories made textiles, or cloth. The factories received cotton harvested by enslaved people in the South. Then factory workers turned the cotton into textiles. The most notable of the textile mills was run by the Amoskeag Manufacturing Company in Manchester. By the early 1900s, it had 17,000 workers. It was the state's largest employer.

Forests continued to play a role in New Hampshire's new economy. In addition to lumber, its factories began to produce paper. One paper factory was in the city of Berlin. The Berlin Mills Company was the world's biggest paper manufacturer by 1917.

Some people in New Hampshire in the 1800s and early 1900s worked in textile mills, including in the Amoskeag Manufacturing Company mill.

MODERN INDUSTRIES

Today manufacturing is still an important part of New Hampshire's economy. But the products have changed. The largest area of manufacturing is smart manufacturing and high technology (SMHT).

People enjoy a variety of winter activities in New Hampshire, including snowshoeing.

SMHT companies use high-tech machines to make parts such as microchips for computers and other electronics.

Tourism is the state's second-largest industry. The White Mountains are one of the biggest attractions. People come to hike, camp, and canoe there. In the winter visitors can ski and snowboard. Resorts along the state's many lakes provide a place for visitors to enjoy the state's natural beauty. Cities along the coast boast beaches and many historic sites.

Health care is another important industry in the state. More than 70,000 people in New Hampshire work in this industry. They perform medical research and care for patients in hospitals and clinics.

STRAIGHT TO THE
SOURCE

People sometimes started working in textile mills at a young age. This was the case for Alice Olivier, who worked at the Amoskeag mills. Olivier said:

> *When I graduated from grammar school at fourteen, in 1930, I got a job in the mill. . . . As a child I used to go and visit my father in the spinning room. You can't hear yourself talk in there, the noise is so loud. So I was petrified when I found out I was going to work in the mills. My mother came with me to the office to get a job. We spoke to the man, and she told him that she preferred that I . . . go where there were only girls. So I got into the cloth room, where it was nice and quiet. . . . I was so happy there. I guess it was the relief of not having to go to those horrible mills that I hated so.*

Source: Randolph Langenbach. "Voices of a Vanished Amoskeag." *American Heritage*, Oct./Nov. 1978, americanheritage.com. Accessed 12 Aug. 2021.

WHAT'S THE BIG IDEA?

Take a close look at this passage. What is the main point Olivier is making about working in mills?

PEOPLE AND PLACES

New Hampshire is one of the least diverse states in the nation. Ninety percent of the population is white people who are not Hispanic or Latino. Four percent are Hispanic or Latino, and 3 percent are Asian. About 2 percent are Black. New Hampshire does not have any federally or state-recognized American Indian tribes. But a few tribes are based in the state, including some from the Abenaki Nation.

Many people live and work in Manchester.

Many New Hampshirites live in cities. The largest city is Manchester. It is located along the banks of the Merrimack River. Some of the state's cities are home to well-respected schools. Dartmouth College is in Hanover. It has been educating students since 1769. The University of New Hampshire is in Durham. It is one of the nation's top research universities.

New Hampshirites have impacted the nation in many ways. Several famous writers have come from New Hampshire. They include novelists J. D. Salinger and Jodi Picoult, as well as poets Robert

IMMIGRANTS

In the state's early history, most people in New Hampshire had roots in England or Scotland. Between 1840 and 1924, thousands of immigrants from Canada, Ireland, Sweden, Germany, Italy, and Greece arrived in New Hampshire. They were often seeking jobs, religious freedom, or safety. In 2018 immigrants accounted for about 6 percent of New Hampshire's population. Most came from India, Canada, China, Nepal, and the Dominican Republic.

A statue of Harriet Wilson stands in Milford.

Frost and E. E. Cummings. Another author from the state was Harriet Wilson. In 1859 she published a novel. It was the first novel written by a Black woman to be published in the United States.

The state was the home of the nation's fourteenth president, Franklin Pierce. He served from 1853 to 1857. It was also the home of multiple astronauts. Alan B. Shepard Jr. grew up in East Derry. In 1961 he became the first American to travel to space. Christa McAuliffe worked as a teacher in Concord. She was aboard the space shuttle *Challenger* in 1986 as the first teacher to go to space. She died when the shuttle exploded

PERSPECTIVES

JEANNE SHAHEEN

Jeanne Shaheen was born in Saint Charles, Missouri, in 1947. She moved to New Hampshire in 1973, where she started a jewelry store. Shaheen was also interested in politics. She won a seat in New Hampshire's state legislature in 1990. She served there until 1996, when she was elected governor of New Hampshire. This made her the state's first female governor. After serving three terms, she stepped down and ran for a seat in the US Senate. She won in 2008. This made her the first female US senator from the state. And it also made her the first woman in the nation to serve as both a governor and a US senator.

soon after the launch, but she inspired many students to enter the field of science.

PLACES

New Hampshire has many historic cities. One of them is Portsmouth. It is located where the Piscataqua River empties into the Atlantic Ocean. Visitors can tour the Strawbery Banke Museum there. Its guides wear historical costumes and show visitors what life was like in Portsmouth 300 years ago.

The Strawbery Banke Museum has houses furnished with items from the 1600s through the 1900s.

Visitors can also travel a walking path called the Portsmouth Harbour Trail. It highlights more than 70 sites that influenced the city. The city is also home to the Black Heritage Trail. This walking tour brings visitors to sites that have played an important role in the Black experience in the state.

Other people come to the state to enjoy the fall colors. Many like to drive on the Kancamagus Highway. It runs for 34.5 miles (55.5 km), winding through the White Mountain National Forest. The drive includes several views of rivers and waterfalls. The area has many trails and campgrounds.

People also admire the state's many covered bridges. Residents began to build them in the early 1800s. The covers protected the wooden bridges from the effects of harsh weather. Today some of these bridges still exist. They are protected by state law, and many are now on the National Register of Historic Places.

Throughout its history New Hampshire has played a unique role in the nation. Today it is a modern, thriving state. Its people, businesses, schools, and natural resources mean it has a lot to offer to visitors and residents alike.

STRAIGHT TO THE
SOURCE

In 2020 Abenaki people started the Abenaki Trails Project. Its goal is to connect the state with its Abenaki roots. As it grows it will highlight important Abenaki places in the state by offering hikes, displays, and historical information. Robert Goodby, an archaeologist working on the project, said:

> *The Native people have always known that they have a long history here and that these sorts of sites exist. For most non-Native people, it's very easy to spend your whole life living in New Hampshire and never really think about the Native presence here, and I think this is a way of bringing that presence into the light, community by community.*

> Source: Chelsea Sheasley. "'We Still Live Here': Native Americans Affirm Their New Hampshire Roots." *Christian Science Monitor*, 15 June 2021, csmonitor.com. Accessed 3 Sept. 2021.

WHAT'S THE BIG IDEA?

Take a close look at this passage. What kind of value does a project like this bring to the community? How is seeing a historical site in person different than reading about it in a book?

IMPORTANT DATES

12,000 years ago
The first people are living in present-day New Hampshire.

1603
British explorer Martin Pring and his crew become the first Europeans known to set foot in New Hampshire.

1629
British colonel John Mason receives a land grant for New Hampshire, sets up a fur trading company, and brings a group of settlers to New Hampshire.

1776
During the Revolutionary War, New Hampshire passes the first state constitution.

1783
Slavery is made illegal in New Hampshire.

1788
New Hampshire delegates vote to ratify the US Constitution on June 21. This makes New Hampshire the ninth state. It is also the vote that makes the Constitution the nation's official law.

1859
New Hampshire native Harriet Wilson becomes the first Black woman in the United States to publish a novel.

1961
New Hampshire native Alan Shepard becomes the first American to go to space.

2018
Immigrants make up approximately 6 percent of New Hampshire's population.

Say What?

Studying a state and its history can mean learning a lot of new vocabulary. Find five words in this book you've never heard before. Use a dictionary to find out what they mean. Then write the meanings in your own words and use each word in a new sentence.

Surprise Me

Chapter Two discusses the history of New Hampshire. After reading this chapter, what questions do you still have about this topic? With an adult's help, find a few reliable sources that can help you answer your questions. Write a paragraph about what you have learned.

Take a Stand

New Hampshire has cities as well as many natural areas. If you spent a vacation in New Hampshire, would you prefer to spend your time in a city or in nature? Why?

You Are There

Chapter Three describes New Hampshire's geography, plants, and animals. Imagine you are traveling in the state. Write a letter to your friends about the trip. What sort of landscapes do you see? What plants and animals have you found in the different regions?

GLOSSARY

erode
to wear away by the movement of wind, water, or other natural forces

export
to ship and sell products to another region or country

immunity
a body's ability to resist a disease through previous exposure to it

land grant
a plot of land given to a person or group for a specific purpose

quarry
an open area where stones or minerals are dug up

ratify
to sign or give formal consent to an agreement or document

shrewd
having sharp powers of judgment

temperate
a climate that does not have extremely hot or cold temperatures

thrifty
having to do with the habit of using what one has carefully and not in excess

ONLINE RESOURCES

To learn more about New Hampshire, visit our free resource websites below.

Visit **abdocorelibrary.com** or scan this QR code for free Common Core resources for teachers and students, including vetted activities, multimedia, and booklinks, for deeper subject comprehension.

Visit **abdobooklinks.com** or scan this QR code for free additional online weblinks for further learning. These links are routinely monitored and updated to provide the most current information available.

LEARN MORE

Bruchac, Joseph. *The Hunter's Promise.* Wisdom Tales, 2015.

Krull, Kathleen. *A Kid's Guide to the American Revolution.* HarperCollins, 2018.

INDEX

About the Author

Kate Conley has been writing nonfiction books for children for more than ten years. When she's not writing, Conley spends her time reading, sewing, and solving crossword puzzles. She lives in Minnesota with her husband and two children.